Werner Bischof

France, 1944.

Werner Bischof

Niklaus Flüeler

AMPHOTO
American Photographic Book Publishing Co., Inc.
Garden City, New York

Werner Bischof
is part of a series entitled
PHOTOGRAPHY: MEN AND MOVEMENTS
Edited by Romeo E. Martinez in cooperation with Max A. Wyss

Library of Congress Catalog Card Number 75-34606
ISBN 0-8174-0318-3

English translation: Maureen Oberli-Turner
Photographs printed by C. J. Bucher, Luzern/Switzerland
Text printed in the United States of America
Werner Bischof's drawings were taken from the sketch books
made between 1943 and 1954.

This book could well have been conceived in a different form than that in which it now appears. It would have been possible, for example, to have arranged the photographs according to their subject matter: children, sufferings of war, countries, landscapes, still lifes, architecture, animals, animals and people, portraits, groups, and people sleeping. It would have been a relatively simple matter to draw conclusions about Werner Bischof's aspirations and inclinations through the subjects that constantly recur throughout his work. Sleep, for example, is a theme that returns continuously in his pictures—the blindly trusting devotion of sleep; the defenselessness of the sleeping human being; the sleep of the just, the wretched, or the troubled; the sleep of forgetfulness; and the hope of an awakening to a better tomorrow, or at least to some tomorrow. This is a subject that appears again and again in Werner Bischof's photographs—a theme which, in itself, provides abundant food for thought and contemplation.

In the case of many other photographers, a thematic grouping of their work would be thoroughly reasonable and justified. With Werner Bischof, however, a chronological arrangement of the pictures comes logically and naturally, for the superficial course of events, the photographer's inner development, the metamorphoses and transformations that took place in the medium of photography between 1939 and 1954, and Werner Bischof's work itself are all closely linked and more mutually dependent than in the case of most other photographers.

To those who did not know Bischof, there would appear to be little connection between his first photographs and the last pictures he took on the Peruvian Plateau.

They are not only representative of two entirely different photographic styles, but they also evidence two completely different ways of seeing and interpreting the world. Nevertheless, hidden links between the first and the last photographs do, in fact, exist. Although the early pictures give little hint as to Werner Bischof's later development, many of the later photographs refer back to the origins—to Bischof's primary intentions and photographic purpose. Had the beginning been other than it was, many of his pictures might have turned out very differently, and many might not have been made at all.

As regards both the formal and the technical aspects of his work, Bischof always remained faithful to his ideals and to the high standards he set for himself. What changed over the years were the themes and style of his pictures; some of these developments verged on the dramatic. A basic, though concealed, continuity remained throughout, however, due partly to the fact that whenever it was possible, Bischof chose his subjects with a view to learning more about the world, mankind, and himself through his photography; this applies equally to the picture of the shell, taken in 1941, and to that of the flute-playing Peruvian boy walking along a road in the Andes, made in 1954.

The task of tracing Werner Bischof's inner development is interesting enough, but it is made still more fascinating by the fact that he exercised a considerable influence on photography itself. It is impossible to divorce the story of his life from the history of photography, even though Bischof did not enter the medium directly and spontaneously. The path that led from the style of photography with which he began to that which finally made him famous was long.

5

Branch with fruit, 1944.

Werner Bischof embarked upon a course of training as a teacher of drawing and sports in Schiers, in the Grisons. He did not stay with this for long, however, and in 1932, he enrolled in the so-called general class at the Kunstgewerbeschule (School of Applied Arts) in Zurich, where he trained in modeling, freehand and machine drawing, nature study, lettering, and perspective. In the same year, he also joined the newly formed photography class founded by Hans Finsler, and in 1936, he graduated with degrees in photography and graphic art.

Bischof learned a great deal at the Kunstgewerbeschule. From Alfred Williman, with whom he studied graphic art, he learned to work creatively with text and pictures, and still more important, he acquired his love of precision, clean and scrupulously executed work, and ethical working principles. From Hans Finsler he received what was possibly the best photographic training available at any school, first and foremost in the technical aspects, as well as in the art of seeing and comprehending what photography really is, what it is capable of, and where its limits lie. From Hans Finsler he also learned that although the formal design of a picture—the angle, cropping, sharpness or unsharpness of focus, motion, and contrast—has an undoubted formal and aesthetic function, it nevertheless takes second place to the picture's statement, which it helps to formulate.

His teachers' methods of instruction and mental attitudes must have been ideal for Werner Bischof's development. Conscientious, almost pedantically devoted to perfection, and gifted with a tireless patience when it came to obtaining the image he saw in his mind's eye, he was an ideal pupil for Williman and Finsler. And if it is true to say

Werner Bischof was born on April 26, 1916, in Zurich, Switzerland, where he lived for a time before moving to the nearby village of Kilchberg. His mother died when he was still an infant, and in 1922, his father moved to Waldshut, just across the German border, where he became director of a pharmaceutical company and where the young Werner attended primary and secondary school. Werner Bischof's relationship with his father was never particularly good, and in 1931, the conflict broke out into the open. Whereas Werner wanted to become a painter, his father aimed at "making something of him" and favored a technical profession. Finally a compromise was reached;

Ba Rau, village in Indochina, 1952.

that Finsler was one of the very few who ventured to the utmost limits of the possibilities offered by photography as early as the twenties, the same certainly applied to Werner Bischof fifteen years later. Finsler noticed early on that Bischof was not only searching for perfection in his pictures but was also intent on comprehending and providing insight into visible phenomena by means of photography. By reducing the objects he photographed to their purest and most basic form, he attempted to penetrate the very essence of things and reveal a clear but hidden law and order in everything he saw. This preoccupation with clarity was not, however, a formalistic end in itself for Bischof, and it would appear that what he was really searching for was insight into his own situation.

"As is usually the case, that which later became clear to Bischof and visible in his work was already present at the beginning in an unconscious form. The unusual thing about Bischof was that he fought and rejected, either intentionally or instinctively, anything and everything that threatened to hinder his growth and development, even if it meant sacrificing material advantages. The work he did in his free time was intensive in the extreme, and he sometimes set himself apparently pointless tasks, which an outsider could well have regarded as childish but which in fact formed the basis of his later work. Material and light are the two components at the root of everything

visible, and Bischof learned to master them in ever-changing variations. But it was organic life—plants, animals, and human beings—that was really closest to him, although he kept this to himself for quite some time.

"In his first semester as a student, he was set the task of taking a picture of something which appealed to him; as his subject, Bischof chose the carved scroll of his violin, which was similar in shape to the shell of a snail. Later, with infinite patience, he took snail shells apart to study their coils and spirals, and he was also fascinated by the coils of ferns as they unfurled. Later still, he portrayed the unfurling of the human fruit. This ever-present unfolding and unfurling was very much a part of Bischof's inner vision, and the spiral may be regarded as the symbol of his growth."[1]

The isolation of the object and the attempt to penetrate the purely material aspect of things with the help of light, thereby revealing something of the essential nature of his subject, were things that fascinated Bischof for many years. "Between 1937 and 1944, when he was working for the Swiss National Exhibition, the magazine *Annabelle*, and textile and other firms, Bischof developed his own style of graphic photography which, in his uncommissioned work, went as far as the decomposition of the object and was indicative of his original desire to paint."[2]

At that time, Bischof had not yet completely relinquished his painting ambitions. Three years after completing his studies at

[1] Hans Finsler, *Werner Bischof, Das photographische Werk,* Pamphlet No. 216, published by the Zurich Kunstgewerbemuseum, p. 5.

[2] Finsler, *op. cit.*, p. 7.

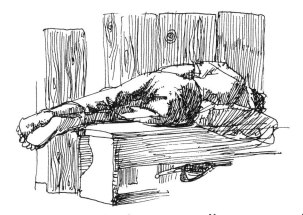

the Kunstgewerbeschule, having worked as a freelance photographer and graphic artist, as an employee with Graphis Publishers in Zurich, and once more as a freelance photographer for the Swiss National Exhibition in Zurich in 1939, Bischof decided for the second time to become a painter. Shortly before the outbreak of World War II he moved to Paris with this end in view, but the war forced him to return to Switzerland where he served in the army for the next three years, as well as worked for the magazine *Du*, which was founded by Arnold Kübler in 1941.

We can only speculate as to how far Bischof would have risen as a painter, and the extent to which his renunciation of a painting career burdened him and influenced his way of photographing. It is quite possible that in the end he was grateful to fate for making him return to Switzerland from Paris. It is impossible to predict whether he would have been successful as a painter. The fact that he was strongly drawn to this art is abundantly clear, and the urge to paint pursued him for eight whole years.

The reason why he eventually gave up the idea of a career as a painter may have been that he was not entirely confident as to his success. Were he still alive, Bischof would now be in his late 50's, a contemporary and competitor of painters such as Lichtenstein, de Staël, Chillida, Tapiès, Manessier, and Bacon, and his work would have been obliged to stand comparison with theirs. But it may also be that he had gradually come to feel that painting was for him an attempt to escape the harsh reality that surrounded him, an attempt to continue along the path upon which he had embarked with photography: the path leading from outward appearances to an inner reality.

Bischof's attitude toward photography appears to have altered with his renunciation of painting. From then on, he identified

interpreting objects in the clearest way possible; it became more and more a means of expression and a way of communicating with his environment. The experience he gained, the human contacts he sought and found, the encounters he made, and the journeys he took all gradually became absorbed into his photography. At the moment Bischof decided finally and irrevocably in favor of photography, the tension within him relaxed for the first time, and a feeling of social responsibility, which he had subconsciously always sought, took control. Photography became a matter of conscience, and he began to think seriously about its position and function in society. It is questionable whether he would ever have found the same commitment in the field of painting.

This inner metamorphosis did not become evident immediately and consistently in the pictures that he made in the following years. Bischof was torn by a curious conflict between his readiness to reveal himself spontaneously and impartially to the world and his attempt to take photographs in the way he had learned and hitherto practiced. Until then, he had portrayed the world as he secretly wished it to be, as a well-ordered cosmos regulated by real but hidden laws. It is characteristic of Bischof that he once said of Japan, "God lives where it is clean." All through his life he sought a well-ordered, contented world, he searched unceasingly for proof of its existence, and he suffered from the fact that reality, with which he had now begun to come to grips, was usually a long way from his ideal.

The reality with which Bischof now became acquainted was the reality of a Europe laid waste by war. In 1945, he traveled

himself far more strongly with the photographic medium, and he turned his attention toward new themes. In 1944, *Du* magazine published a special issue devoted to the theme of "The Disabled Person," in which all the photographs were by Werner Bischof and represented a "definite turn toward the problematic human interest reportage" (Manuel Gasser). Photography no longer served Bischof solely as a means of

through France, Germany, and Holland, and the following year, he was commissioned by the Don Suisse, Swiss Relief, to visit Italy and Greece. In autumn 1947, he traveled to Vienna, Hungary, and Rumania. In 1948, he visited eastern and northern Europe, including Hungary, Czechoslovakia, Poland, Finland, Sweden, and Denmark. In May of the same year, he married his wife, Rosellina, and moved to England where he entered into a permanent working relationship with *Picture Post,* and the *Observer.* In 1949, Werner Bischof also became a member of Magnum, to which Henri Cartier-Bresson, David Seymour, Robert Capa, George Rodger, and Ernst Haas also belonged. His first son, Marc, was born in 1950, and in the same year, he traveled to Italy, Sardinia, Paris, and Iceland.

The pictures he made between 1944 and 1950 are characterized by a curious duality, which Bischof himself probably felt very acutely at the time. His growing participation in reality, his sympathy toward his fellow human beings, which he had now ceased to hide, and his social commitment were incompatible with the emotional distance he had acquired. His faith in the lawful, ordered nature of the world was shaken and undermined by what he saw around him. He was deeply moved by what he observed and photographed on his journeys through eastern Europe, and he must have experienced a genuine disgust and moral aversion to what he now encountered. In-

wardly, he rejected what he saw; it was as if a part of his very being was being wrenched out of him, and sensitive as he was, he must in some way have felt a sense of responsibility for the war and its consequences. Possibly as a means of self-protection and a defense of his belief in an ordered world, Bischof sought comfort more and more often in the hidden beauty present in less terrible themes in his photography. Examples of this are the pictures of the tearful Hungarian child (1947), the girl with the birds (1948), the Rumanian beggar (1948), and the herd of reindeer in northern Finland (1948). Bischof probably sought this compensation intentionally to enable him to carry on taking photographs of the things that shocked and hurt him, and this made his work vulnerable to the criticism of aestheticism for many years. But Bischof needed time to come to terms with the reality of the world and to assimilate and digest the events, experiences, and impressions that stormed in upon his consciousness. The fact that this took some time was due not to a flaw in his character but to the very essence of his nature, for he was a sensitive, highly vulnerable person. His horror at the misery and wretchedness of war and its aftermath was genuine and deeply felt, and this horror was revealed again and again in his pictures through a perceptible restraint and diffidence.

Between 1944 and 1950, Werner Bischof had another experience that impressed him deeply and forced him to reconsider his attitude toward photography: He came into contact with photojournalism. Due to his education and his natural inclination to probe deeply into things, Bischof had, until now, endeavored to express as much as possible through a single image and to concentrate and condense his statement; thus each one of his pictures was an attempt at a synthesis. His travels, his contact with the people at Magnum, the stylistic developments in the whole conception and design of the big illustrated magazines, the increased amount of space they now allotted to photography, and the necessity of working quickly and documenting comprehensively all combined to force Bischof to reconsider his way of working and his relationship to the picture. A single image, which represents the attempt at a synthesis, and a series of pictures, which purport to take apart and analyze a situation in order to reach a synthesis from that basis, are, although perhaps similar at base, nevertheless dissimilar enough to demand a totally different approach. Bischof grasped this immediately when he joined Magnum in 1949, and from this moment on, his pictures took on another aspect.

The pictures he took in India, among them those of the starvation areas in the province of Bihar which he made for *Life* in January 1951, reveal a Bischof transformed in many ways. The reportage takes the form of a picture story, and the images have a more direct and immediate impact than his previous photographs had had. This is partly due to his different way of photographing and approaching his theme, and partly to the fact that Bischof had now learned to retain his composure no matter what confronted him. This does not mean

that he no longer sympathized with what he saw and photographed, on the contrary; but the pictures taken in this period convey the impression that he was less tortured and terrorized by his experiences than he had been previously when taking pictures of suffering and misery. In addition to this, Bischof was now confronted with an exotic and completely different way of life in India.

At the same time, the emphasis he had placed on technical perfection, design, and the direction and distribution of light now shifted onto the subject—the theme and content of the picture. His preoccupation with the subject began to take over from his obsession with form, and the journalistic presentation of a theme became more important to him than formal perfection. This did not, however, result in a decrease in quality, for even in the most difficult and fleeting situations, Bischof hardly ever produced a mediocre picture.

The strict, formal education he had received from Williman and Finsler and his long technical and aesthetic photographic practice now started to pay off. Bischof had acquired a photographic culture (in the sense that we speak of a culinary or a linguistic culture), which had become an integral part of his equipment and which never left him, although he did not think about it consciously. This left him with more time and inner calm to devote to intensive study of the subjects of his reportages.

What has been said about the pictures of the starvation areas applies equally to the other photographs he took in India. Here, too, the story-telling series replaced the single, carefully composed, synthesizing image. Bischof's portrayal of India is made up of a whole series of photographs that

came an integral part of his nature, did not, however, entirely oust his secret love of form. Through his preoccupation with formal perfection, Bischof continued to express his belief in a hidden, reasoned order inherent in the world, and since he steadfastly refused to relinquish this belief, his reportages, or the supplements to them, repeatedly contained pictures that circled around the themes of substance, form, and light.

In India, the Observatory in Jaipur provided Bischof with an ideal subject, for in it he found a theme that held a special fascination, an object that was more than mere form, a sculpture with a formal purity that also expressed something about the spirit and beliefs of a whole people. Bischof had not given up the attempt—and in fact, he never gave it up—to express and portray the essence of an object in a visual form and to reach out to an element of truth behind the mere realistic likeness through the medium of photography.

In June 1951, Werner Bischof flew directly from India to Japan, where his wife joined him from Switzerland for Christmas. Werner and Rosellina Bischof lived in Japan for about a year, and the result of this stay was not, as previously, a series of reportages, but a book. This book was really an attempt to comprehend and portray the origins, traditions, and developments of a whole nation. Bischof had not planned his journey to Japan in advance; it resulted from a commission by *Life* that took him to Korea for a reportage on the war and the wretchedness of the refugees. He was thus ill-prepared for his confrontation with Japan, and he was immediately excited and fascinated by the country. Much of what he saw and felt there must have been very

combine to present a picture of the country as he saw and perceived it. Here, too, the reportage-like form of the presentation in no way detracts from the flawless quality of the photography. Bischof always took his time when taking photographs, even when he was obliged to react at lightning speed; and he was unusually economical in his use of film. The time the majority of photographers used to shoot roll after roll of film, from which they later selected the best images, was employed by Bischof to establish the exact angle, composition, and lighting.

The journalistic way of thinking and working, which Bischof acquired in an astonishingly short time and which quickly be-

much in accordance with his previous perceptions and experiences. In portraying Japan, he also portrayed himself, because his own sensibility and his relationship with the world, people, and things was similar to Japan's sensibility and mood. The photographs Werner Bischof took of Japan still take their place among the pictures that express the essence of Japan most truly, even though over 24 years have passed since they were taken.

Another reason why Bischof's stay in Japan was so satisfying to him was that it was the first time that he had had a chance to make a large-scale, well-balanced reportage on a whole country and a whole people, in peace and quiet, and with enough time at his disposal; added to this, the country offered much that delighted his feeling for form. At the same time, he was aware of the danger that lay for him in the purity of the country's architecture and man-made objects, the formal perfection of the ever-present ceremony, and the formality of the people's manners and customs. The country's fascination and compatibility with his own nature finally obliged him to tear himself away from Japan virtually by force.

Viewed as a whole, the pictures he took in Japan would appear to be less dramatic, turbulent, and agitated than those taken in India. This impression is, however, somewhat misleading, and it is perhaps important to distinguish the drama of the theme itself from that of the inner tension with which a photographer may approach his subject. In India, the scenes and events with which he was confronted were expressed directly by Bischof in reportage form; in Japan, on the other hand, Bischof tried once again to express the dramatically perceived tension between tradition and change, ceremony and suppressed vitality, and formal consciousness and threatening chaos in the form of a single picture. Although it may not be evident at first glance, some of the Japan photographs radiate an almost threatening stillness; it is the calm before the storm.

Perhaps it was a good thing that Bischof visited Korea three times during his stay in Japan, and that he subsequently went to Hong Kong and Indochina to make war reportages for *Paris Match*, for this forced him to face up to a different kind of reality—the reality of a new war and its victims. It is striking how often and how ardently Bischof photographed children during this period, and how different these pictures are from the photographs of children he took shortly after World War II. Bischof had always been interested in children, but in spite of this, they had always tended to assume the nature of studio objects in his pictures; to him, they represented unspoiled nature, "the human being to come." His whole attitude toward children had been burdened by his search for the mysterious laws of the macro- and microcosmos. Now, however, all that fell away, and Bischof occupied himself directly and immediately with the fate of these war children; and he did so with such an intensity that when we look at these photographs, we cannot help wondering spontaneously what happened to the child in the picture, if it is still alive, what it looks like now, and whether its circumstances have changed for the better. We have only supposition to go on, but I personally believe that Bischof, himself only recently a father, saw his own child in all these children, and that he felt the same physical and spiritual sympathy toward the children he photographed that he felt toward his own child. Thus, and only thus, can we explain the forceful impact of these photographs. In images like these, photography attains the sublime quality that cannot be explained in terms of technical skill or the laws of aesthetics. How they occur, however, remains one of the unsolved secrets of photography.

Shortly before the Christmas of 1952, Werner and Rosellina Bischof returned to Switzerland, and from then until the autumn of 1953, Bischof sorted and worked on his Asian photographs and prepared for the publication of his book on Japan. In September, he sailed to New York to make preparations for a car journey through Central and South America. The United States came as a shock to Bischof; New York terrified and crippled him. "The impression which New York made on Werner Bischof could have been foreseen: to a man so closely bound to nature and the subtlest impulses of the human spirit, the steel and concrete monster of Manhattan could only have seemed terrifying and unnatural . . . In this city, the human being is present only in terms of that which his brain has designed and his machines constructed, in

the stone and steel monstrosities which tower so high above him that his tiny figure can barely hold its own beneath the Babylonian towers which he has erected. And when, notwithstanding, man does appear upon the scene, it is not as the master and beneficiary of this world which he has created, but as a prisoner, a trapped animal trying desperately to break out of its cage of tangled steel wires."[3]

Bischof took but few photographs in the United States, and the existing pictures show streets, roadway crossings, concrete, forbidding façades, and a Manhattan filled with smoke and fumes. He could glean nothing from the ugliness and brutality of the country, and he seemed unable to perceive its beauty. Finsler's remark about Bischof's work is particularly applicable to his American visit: "In all Werner Bischof's work, the consciousness of a law and order in human existence is perceptible. It is a criterion, a module present in all his pictures, which also figures as the criterion of what he portrays. Often, though, the criterion is visible only in deformation, in the contravention of a basic law. The anamorphotic reflection of the strict, rigid form of a skyscraper in the polish of a car, for example, takes on the appearance of a symbol of a section of our modern life."[4]

Bischof's sole aim in the United States was to establish contact with the editors of magazines before continuing by car to Mexico, Panama, Peru, Chile, and finally Tierra del Fuego. A commission from *Fortune* made it necessary for him to prolong his

[3] Manuel Gasser, *Werner Bischof, Unterwegs,* Zurich, 1957, p. 57.

[4] Manuel Gasser, *op. cit.,* p. 76.

3

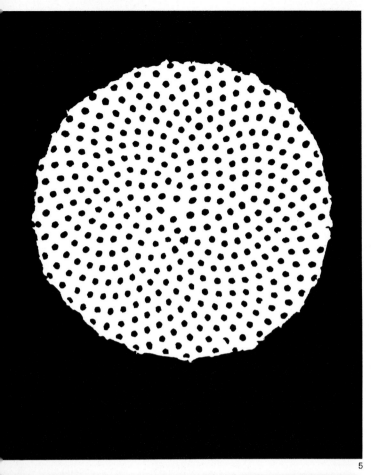

5

7

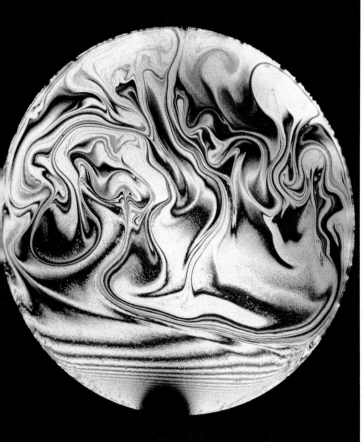

6

8

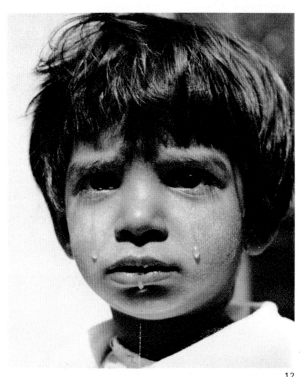

12

13

14

15

17

18

19

21

22

24

23

26

28

27

29

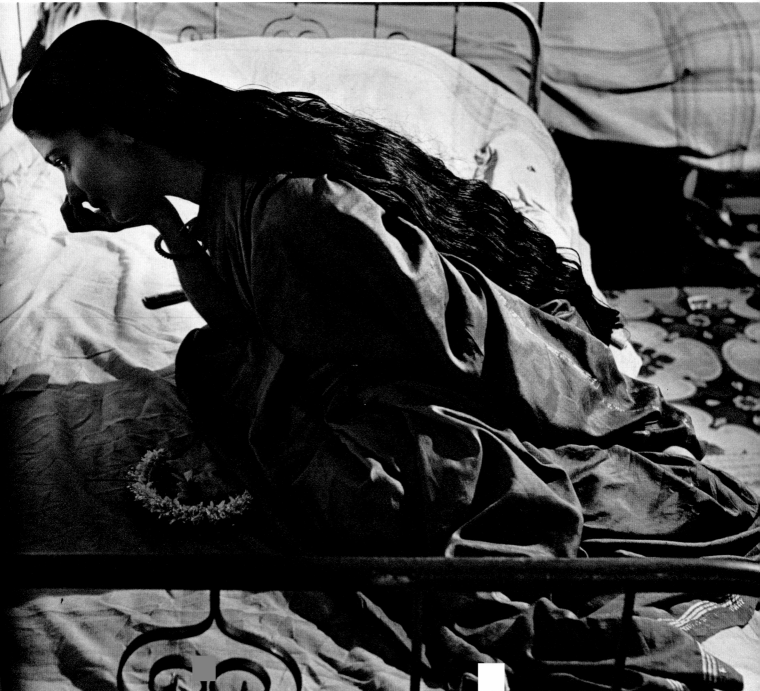

38

39

40

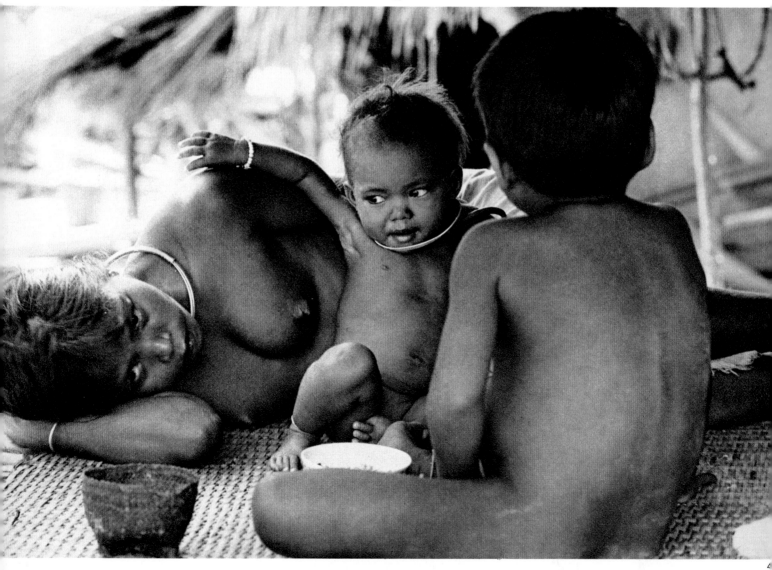

44

45

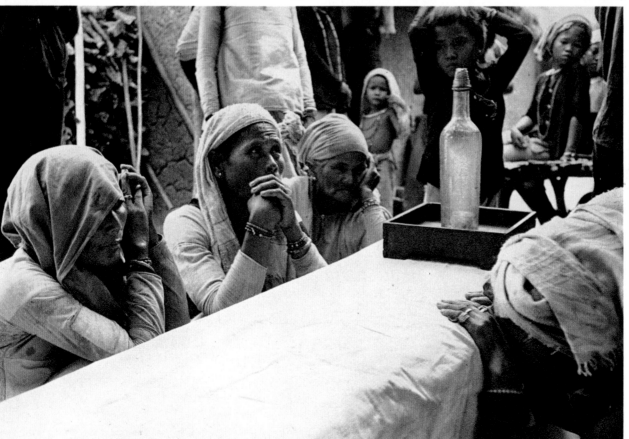

46

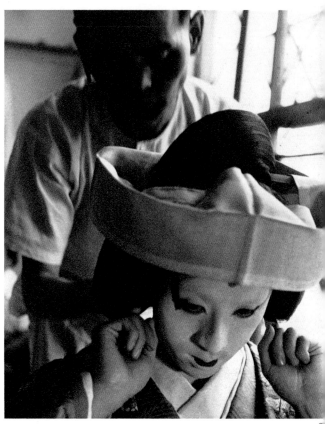

69

70

71

72

73

Ba Rau, village in Indochina, 1952.

stay, however, and at the end of the year, he was joined by Rosellina in St. Louis. In the beginning of February 1954, they traveled together to Mexico, from where Bischof flew on to Panama for *Life* and subsequently to Lima, Peru, and Santiago, Chile, to work on the Magnum reportage "Generation Women." His wife, who was expecting their second child, flew back to Switzerland. After spending his thirty-eighth birthday in Lima, Bischof visited the Inca city of Machu Picchu, near Cuzco, before flying back once more to Lima to meet the geologist Ali de Szepessy, whom he had met previously in Zurich. "On May 14, Werner Bischof, Ali de Szepessy and a driver left for Trujillo, from where they continued along an Andes road, which was considered to be 'neither better nor worse than most roads in the area.' Two days later, their car was found wrecked at the bottom of a gorge. No one knows how the accident happened. The time is assumed to have been around noon on May 16, 1954."[5]

The pictures Bischof took during the last four or five months of his life are beginnings and fragments of larger, unfinished reportages. After his stay in the United States, Central and South America came as a relief to him, and he felt himself once again among human beings and in contact with nature. A strange wanderlust overcame him, his pictures took on a quality of turbulence and unrest (Bischof had begun to experiment with unsharpness and blur), and an Arriflex, with which he had intended to make a film in Venezuela, was found in his luggage.

It is pointless to speculate about how Bis-

chof would have continued to develop, what his work would have looked like five or six years later, and how deep his commitment to photography would have become. On the evening before the journey that was to lead to his death, Bischof conversed late into the night with friends on the subject of Magnum, an organization that had become too commercial for his taste and of whose success he was somewhat afraid. He had never regarded Magnum merely as a photo agency and sales organization but as a working community of photographers whose responsibility it was to set an example through their work—an example not merely of how to take first-class photographs but also of how to speak to people through the medium of photography and to communicate what was important to the photographer.

It is possible that Bischof would have left Magnum sooner or later as a polite but definite protest, and that he would have continued along his own individual, independent path—or so, at least, the inner unrest of his last photographs would lead us to suppose. For in spite of his undoubted charm and the politeness always present in his relations with other people, there was nevertheless a trace of bad temper in Bischof's makeup, which was sometimes mistaken for conceit but which was in fact something quite different—an egoism directed toward the interests of the thing itself, toward the service of photography as he understood it. With his increasing political and social consciousness, this vital ill-humor might well have increased too, and it is possible that Bischof gradually would have liberated himself from all his ties so as to be able to express himself freely through his photography.

[5] Hans Finsler, "Das Bild der Photographie," *Du*, Vol. 24, March 1964. p. 53.

Houseboat on the Sumida River, Tokyo, Japan, 1951.

There is no shortage of testimonials to Werner Bischof's humaneness, seriousness, conscientiousness, readiness to help, thirst for experience, purity of conviction, and refusal to compromise. "His seriousness, moral fiber, and the combination of tenderness, severity, sovereignty, and humility were admired by all who knew him."[1]

The respect Bischof enjoyed during his lifetime was in danger of changing into hero-worship after his death, particularly in Switzerland where he was the nation's greatest and most famous photographer at the time of his death. Bischof himself would certainly have been the first to reject this, for even though he regarded photography as a means of communicating with his fellow man—a language in which he could express himself far better than in words—and even though he was dependent on making friends through his photography, he was at the same time irritated by any overflattering admiration of his work. Exaggerated admiration was incompatible with his introverted, shy, and sometimes uncertain manner, which was an integral part of his nature.

This is not the place for a study of Werner Bischof's character, for this is only worthwhile as long as it contributes to an understanding of his photography; all the rest is a private and personal matter. The question of Bischof's importance to the medium of photography as a whole, and the position his work occupies in its history, is far more important. Here, too, there is no simple and direct answer, and the best we can do is to try to elucidate the working conditions and situation of photography between 1936 and 1954 with a view to a more or less valid judgment and appraisal of Bischof's work.

[1] Finsler, *Werner Bischof*, p. 5.

First, we must remember that Bischof had the advantage of being one of the few European photographers of the postwar period to have received photographic training. In addition, photographers in Switzerland were able to continue working comparatively undisturbed during the war—something which was impossible in most other countries. Also, the founding of the magazine *Du* in 1941 gave Bischof an opportunity to publish his work, a chance enjoyed by few other photographers at the time; and his collaboration with Arnold Kübler, the founder and first editor of *Du*, provided him with further impetus and inspiration.

During the years immediately after the war, a temporary and undefined solidarity developed among the few really good photographers in Europe, and this had a variety of causes. The number of photographers who had been well known before the war was extremely small, and hardly any new photographers were trained during the war years. The few photographers of the younger generation found immediate and spontaneous contact with their older colleagues; they spoke the same professional language, although with a different accent; they had the same ambitions and worries; they were documenting the same war and the fate of the same world, regardless of whether they were working in France, the United States, Germany, Eastern Europe, or Greece; and together they aspired to build up something new. In addition, they were all convinced of the power, impact, and incorruptibility of photography.

The enthusiasm in the photography of the postwar period was encouraged by the growing demand for photographs in newspapers and magazines. The press, which was gradually recovering from the war and

which was being rebuilt from the very beginning in many countries, gained more and more confidence in the effectiveness of the photographic image and allotted it more and more space in their publications. The situation was further influenced by two other developments: The position now occupied by photography in the press resulted in more generous layouts; and this in its turn led to an upsurge in photojournalism, which was now being rediscovered and was starting to enjoy a new popularity.

The American magazines had a determining influence on this development. Magazine design in Europe in 1947 had remained fixed at approximately the same point that it had reached in Germany in 1929, and this meant that photography's main purpose was to illustrate the text and impress the reader by its visual appeal. Now, however, photography began to take over a large part of the actual communication, which had hitherto traditionally been left to the text, and in order to fulfill this new role satisfactorily, it was necessary for the photographers to adopt a journalistic approach and working method. This resulted, naturally, in a departure from the single, impactful photograph and the advent of the picture story. The presentation of the picture story required space—more space than for a mere series of photographs placed one after another because some images were more important than others to the story's statement. Thus, this new medium of photojournalism called for layouts using half, full, quarter, or double pages according to the story's content and requirements. Although the presentation of picture stories demanded more space than had been usual, it was generally agreed that the generous disposition was justified and that photography deserved its new significance.

For the few photographers working in Europe at the time, this was truly a golden age, and since there was enough work available and nothing to stop them from expressing themselves freely through their pictures in newspapers and magazines, the professional jealousy and competition, which are so commonplace among photographers today, were unknown at the time. In fact, the euphoria of the period is indirectly to blame for the situation in photography today; for the boom that the medium experienced in the fifteen years following the war contributed to its rise in stature to a promising profession, and the number of photographers increased accordingly. The fact that the magazines were to change considerably in the coming years, and that many of them were to fold altogether, could not be foreseen at the time. In addition, a growing mistrust in the statement value of photography led gradually to a restraint in the use of the spacially demanding medium in newspapers and magazines, and

layout. In addition, his work for *Du* brought him into contact with the world of journalism. Shortly after the war, it was also an advantage to possess a Swiss passport, and the position in which photography found itself at that time represented yet another advantage for Bischof.

All this would have been to no avail, however, if Bischof had lacked certain personal qualities. He was versatile, intelligent, and quick to learn—as he had proved by the speed with which he had mastered the changeover to photojournalism—and the more he lost his reservations and his awkwardness, the more his pictures gained in depth and breadth. He was also one of the first to grasp instinctively how to work in color and that color photography has laws different from those of black-and-white. Additionally, he realized at once that although some subjects are better suited to black-and-white, color can, in certain circumstances, endow the object photographed with an entirely different, and sometimes unforeseen, significance. Bischof, not content with the mere awareness of this fact, also developed a genuine facility in color work, and the color pictures he took between 1948 and 1954 can easily hold their own against the best color photographs in a similar style even today. How far Bischof would have progressed in the field of color is a matter for speculation, but when we look at his last pictures, we can assume that he would have developed a personal style and a conception of color in accordance with his concept of light, form, and texture, and that his color work would probably have been comparable today with the pictures of, say, Ernst Haas.

One way of establishing Werner Bischof's importance to photography as a whole is to

this same mistrust induced editors and art directors to "edit" the pictures more frequently, i.e., to crop and arrange them for the purpose of making their own statements rather than those of the photographers.

But to return to Bischof. It is clear that in the situation just described, he had an advantage in many ways: He was one of the few photographers who had received a training in the medium; he had continued working throughout the war; he had no trouble publishing his pictures; and due to his previous training and experience as a graphic artist, he understood something about design and

consider the influence he had on the photography of his day and the photographers who succeeded him. One thing is certain: Today's middle generation of photographers was greatly impressed by Bischof and did its best to follow his example. Bischof also had a strong influence upon the photography of Italy and Sweden, and for some time, there was hardly a photographer in these countries who did not follow minutely Bischof's work and publications. His influence on French photography was less direct, for his pictures of eastern Europe were the first to become known in France and his earlier works were only recognized some time later. It was not until after he became a member of Magnum in 1949 that Bischof's pictures began to appear in French magazines and to exercise an influence on the country's photography. In the end, his influence on French photography was probably greater than that which he had on the other Magnum photographers, for Cartier-Bresson, Capa, Rodger, Seymour, and Haas were all older than Bischof and had already formed their own style. What Bischof did show the people at Magnum, however, was his awareness of form and the aesthetics of the picture, his own high standard of technical perfection, and above all, his sensitive feeling for light. Cartier-Bresson wrote: "His photographs are structured, above all, around light—light that is supple, insinuating, and definite, but not harsh. This sensitivity to the

delicacy of light combined with his human understanding and tenderness characterize the poetic photography of Werner Bischof."[2]

His pictures of starvation in India would appear to have had the greatest influence on photography, for his way of approaching the theme, the style of the images, the choice of angle, and the cropping have been

[2] Henri Cartier-Bresson in *Werner Bischof, Querschnitt*, Zurich, 1961, p. 8. The original French quotation reads: "Ses photographies s'organisent avant tout par rapport à la lumière, lumière réfléchie, insinuante, ferme, mais sans brutalité. Un sens delicat de la lumière joint à une compréhension humaine et une tendresse souvent bouleversante caractérisent toute la poesie de Werner Bischof."

imitated by many other photographers in similar and different situations—an indication that they learned to see in a manner not unlike Bischof's own. The same applies, on a smaller scale, to his pictures of Japan, the United States, and South America.

Bischof's most enduring influence, however, was undoubtedly exercised by his books, which were easier to acquire for those interested in photography than single issues of *Du, Paris Match, Fortune,* or *Life.* Bischof was one of the first to achieve through his books something many other photographers had only dreamed of: works complete in themselves, in which text, pictures, and design supplemented each other to create a synthesis that could never be reached by photography alone. This was possible for Bischof due to his training as a graphic artist, which enabled him to design his Japan book himself. Had he lived longer, he would probably have written his own texts for his books and supplemented them with his drawings. At least his comprehensive notes and diaries and his countless sketchbooks give rise to the supposition that Bischof had this in mind.

In one sense, a book was a way for Bischof to escape from the endless discussions with editors and art directors. Although he lived during a time in which the photographer enjoyed a certain respect and photography was taken at its face value, he was nevertheless irritated by the way in which certain editors treated his pictures. Basically, his irritation was justified, but the editors usually had the last word, and he was obliged to grit his teeth and bear it. He was in the right because he understood considerably more about the technique and aesthetics of photography than most of the newspapermen and photographers with

whom he dealt, and because he conceived his photographs in such a way as to render any subsequent cropping or other alterations unnecessary and superfluous. Apart from this, the standards he set for himself in regard to his prints and enlargements were so high that only a few people were in the position to appreciate them fully, since most viewers were unable to conceive of the work that had gone into them. Bischof spent whole nights in the laboratory in order to achieve just the right shade of gray or silver, an essential part of his pictures. The relentless, uncompromising precision of the laboratory work with which Bischof perfected his photographs often drove his collaborators almost to despair, and one of the difficulties of reproducing his pictures exactly as he had conceived them is that the art of enlarging has, to a great extent, been lost.

It is understandable that he had few friends among editors and art directors, and it is questionable whether he would have seen eye-to-eye with the newspapers and magazines of the sixties. Their attitude toward photography had already begun to change, and we cannot help wondering how Bischof would have fared if he had continued to work for the press. Perhaps he would finally have given up photography and become a painter.

There can be no doubt that Werner Bischof occupied an important, and perhaps even determining, place in the history of photography. In spite of this, some of his pictures are difficult to comprehend, and although they are necessary to consider for a full understanding of his development, they tend to leave us cold and give the impression of being antiquated, awkward, and detached. These are the photographs Bischof made in the years immediately following the war, and the question is, Where does the fault lie? With Bischof, with ourselves, or with some outside factor? The answer, as is usually the case, is that it lies with all three.

Photography represents, among other things, an expression of the taste of a certain period, and a photograph is inescapably tied to the era in which it was made. This is not a value judgment; it is simply a statement of fact that explains why the inner relationship of the viewer to a picture can change over the years. Moreover, each individual "reads" an image differently according to his interests and education. Bischof's last pictures, i.e., the pictures taken after 1950, are closer to us today; this can be understood principally in terms of time. In a few years time, our attitude toward Bischof's earlier pictures will probably have changed because the aesthetics of the war and postwar years will then be more readily acceptable. Perhaps by then the position of Bischof's earlier photographs within the framework of the history of the aesthetics of photography—which has, incidentally, yet to be written—will be more precisely defined; thus it may be possible to view his work with less prejudice from this greater distance. This certainly applies to the earlier pictures in all their aspects, from the flawlessness of both exposure and laboratory technique to the perfection of the prints and enlargements.

In future anthologies of Bischof's work, certain pictures will probably be omitted since with growing experience, more precise criteria for photographic criticism, and the quantitative increase of good photographs, corrections in the evaluation of Werner Bischof's collected work will almost certainly be necessary; for it is not only the way in which pictures are seen and read that changes—the absolute value of an image also rises or falls before it finally finds its correct place. A photograph can be—in the objective as well as the subjective sense—a moving document of the present, the aesthetic qualities of which become fully evident only later. It can change from a picture once considered beautiful to a mere example of a certain style in the history of photography, or it may be of a lesser aesthetic quality but still remain an historically valuable document—the list could be continued almost indefinitely. This selective process applies as much to Bischof's photographs as to any others, but we should not forget to add that by far the greater part of his work will undoubtedly stand the test of time and selection.

The reason for a certain alienation between some of Bischof's pictures and today's viewer may be our changed way of seeing, which has been brought about in no small measure by the changes in photography itself. The use of extreme focal-length lenses, from the fisheye to the high-power tele, has indirectly reshaped our observation, and we have become spoiled. Work with lenses of unusual focal lengths has laws other than those applying to normal lenses, for the latter force a direct confrontation and exclude all technically determined dramatization. Furthermore, the high-sensitivity films with which today's photographers so successfully bluff their public were not known in Bischof's day. All the same, it is questionable whether extreme focal lengths and high-sensitivity films would have been compatible with Bischof's needs, for his straightforward approach to his themes—his way of encountering his subjects on a man-to-man level and of portraying the human condition as it really is—gives rise to the supposition that he would have regarded the newer equipment and film material produced by the photographic industry with at least a certain reserve. It is even possible that it is just this conservatism which will prove to be Bischof's greatest contribution to photography.

There is not much more to be said about Werner Bischof. Compared to that of other photographers of the same stature, his work is not particularly prolific. The fact that he had such an important influence on the photography of his time, despite the shortness of his life and the comparatively small amount of work he produced, has already made him an authoritative figure in the history of photography. Bischof has been somewhat neglected in the past few years, and we have lost sight of him to a certain extent. It is fairly certain, however, that he will continue to influence the photography of tomorrow in some way or other. Maybe all that is required is a greater distance and a better overall view of photography as a whole, and perhaps a standard for photographic criticism, which has yet to be established—we shall see. In any case, and whatever happens, the rediscovery of Werner Bischof cannot be far off.

Cuzco, Peru, 1954.

South American Indian woman at the market, Pisac, Peru, 1954.

Captions

1 Fashion photograph, taken in connection with an exhibition, around 1940.

2 Plant photogram, 1939.

3 Nude, 1939.

4 Argonaut shell and snail shell, 1941.

5 Seed base, 1941.

6 Soap bubble, 1942.

7 Projection through the lens, 1936.

8 Overlapping of two wave groups in mercury, 1944.

9 Ruins, Hamburg, 1945.

10 Parliament Buildings in Berlin, 1945. Pictures 9 and 10 were taken during the first journey to Germany, which Werner Bischof made with his friend Emil Schulthess for the magazine *Du*.

11 Floods in Hungary, 1947. In 1947, huge floods of water broke through the dam in the Theiss in eastern Hungary. This picture was first published in a special issue of *Du* entitled "Eastern Europe Today."

12 Hungarian child, 1947.

13 Peasants' inn in the Hungarian Puszta, 1948.

14 In the ruins of Danzig, 1945.

15 On a farm near Cracow, Poland, 1948. The wall paintings of decorative folklore motifs are typical. "The walls of the houses are freshly whitewashed every year. The brushes are made from hair cut from horses' tails, and pictures are painted on the freshly whitewashed walls."

16 In the old part of Warsaw, 1948. "At the entrance to a cellar used for living purposes. The room contained two iron bedsteads, and the scanty light entered through the bay window and fell on a bunch of white marguerites. Although modern blocks of flats with gardens are available for employees of the state, thousands of children still grow up in these dark and wretched dwelling places."

17 Rumanian beggar on a market place in Transylvania, 1947.

18 Rumanian peasant near Jassy, 1947.

19 Peasant girl with her trousseau, Rumania, 1947.

20 Herd of reindeer in northern Finland, 1948. "Swift reindeer being herded into the corral."

21 Monte Cassino, Italy, 1946. A peasant woman in front of the completely devastated monastery of Monte Cassino.

22 Italian peasant's kitchen, Tuscany, 1946.

23 Sacristan, Tuscany, 1946.

24 Gypsy girl, Italy, 1947.

25 Winter on Peloponnesus, Greece, 1946.

26–29 In Greece, 1946. Photographs 25–29 were taken on a journey which Werner Bischof made for the Don Suisse.

30 Makeup being applied to a Kathakali dancer in India, 1952. The dancer embodies Krishna. The picture was taken as part of a large-scale reportage on the Kathakali Dances.

31 Indian dancer dressing first thing in the morning. "The morning toilet is a ritual. Anjali Hora chooses her clothes according to the day, the hour, the weather, and her mood. Today is the day of the jasmine fragrance, and she will wear a diadem of fresh jasmine flowers." The picture is part of a reportage on Anjali Hora, an Indian temple dancer.

32 Hunger in Bihar, India, 1951.

33 Hunger in India—exhaustion on the streets of Patna, 1951.

34 Begging for corn, Patna, 1951. Pictures 32, 33, 34, 38, and 39 were taken in the Patna starvation areas and first appeared in *Life* in 1951. These pictures resulted in the grant of a large dispatch of corn to the suffering Indian population by the American Congress.

35–37 In a Madras temple, India, 1952. Unlike our churches, which are usually empty on weekdays, the temples in Asia are a focal point of daily life.

38 A consignment of corn arrives in a village in the province of Bihar, India, 1951.

39 Girls from a village near Patna, India, 1951.

40 Children in Hanoi, Indochina, 1952.

41 Mother and child in Ba Rau, Indochina, 1952. Werner Bischof spent three weeks in Ba Rau, an out-of-the-way village on the railway track between Saigon and Nha Trang, during his stay in Indochina. He lived with the natives and was able to draw and photograph them as he pleased. The train on which he traveled was one of the few armored trains that ran between Saigon and Nha Trang and was regularly blown up by the Viet Minh. The pictures first appeared in *Paris Match*.

42 In the Hanoi Museum, Indochina, 1952.

43 In an overcrowded train between Saigon and Nha Trang, Indochina, 1952.

44 Gambling and opium in Lai Chan, Indochina, 1952. Werner Bischof was confined indoors in Lai Chan for three weeks during the monsoon rains.

45 Prisoners of war in the Red River Delta, Indochina, 1952.

46 Burial ceremony in Ba Rau, Indochina, 1952.

47 Returning from market, Ba Rau, Indochina, 1952.

48 In the streets of Hong Kong, 1952.

49 Food coupons for refugees, Hong Kong, 1952.

50 Refugee family from Shanghai, Hong Kong, 1952.

51 Refugee child on his mother's back, Hong Kong, 1952.

52 Sleeping peasant in Kau Sai, on an island near Hong

Kong, 1952.

53 Ricksha in Hong Kong, 1952. During the years following Mao Tse-tung's victory in 1949, hundreds of refugees arrived in Hong Kong every day for care and accommodation. Werner Bischof visited Hong Kong in 1952. The pictures he took there were first published in *Paris Match* and later in *Life, Illustrated,* and other magazines.

54 Korean boy among American soldiers, Pusan, 1951.

55–57 War children in Seoul, Korea, 1951.

58 Refugee, Seoul, Korea, 1951. In 1951, Werner Bischof visited Korea with the American army as a war correspondent and photographed the civilian population and children behind their own front lines. The story, which first appeared in *Life,* took on the appearance of a reportage against war.

59 Shinto priests returning from morning devotions through the snow-covered courtyard of the Meiji Shrine, Tokyo, 1951.

60 The "tomaye," an ancient sign on the Bugaku drum, symbolizes the motion and revolution of the universe and has been adopted by Shintoism. 1951.

61 Memorial temple for the war victims. The devastated exhibition building over which the atom bomb exploded in Hiroshima is retained as a landmark. Hiroshima, 1951.

62 Shinto priests in the Meiji Shrine, Tokyo, 1951.

63 The Kabuki actor Bondo Mitsugoro applying his makeup, Tokyo, 1951.

64 In Kabuki plays, all the roles are played by men, even those of geishas. Tokyo, 1951.

65 Chorus in the No Theater, Tokyo, 1951. A group of singers sits at the side of the rectangular stage, which is undecorated, symbolizing a room or even a whole province, and a single step may symbolize a journey.

66 The Kabuki actor Bondo Mitsugoro praying before the small altar in his dressing room before his entrance on the stage, Tokyo, 1951.

67 Mitsugoro being dressed as Hero, Tokyo, 1951. The mask-like face makeup, known as Kumadori, expresses anger, jealousy, or some other emotion, according to its form and color.

68 The Emperor Hirohito and his wife on their first visit to Hiroshima after the atom bomb catastrophe, 1951.

69 The Japanese army on maneuver, 1951.

70 One of the few survivors of August 6, 1943, taken in Hiroshima in 1951. He was only one mile away from the center of the explosion when he attempted to seek protection in the doorway of a house. The scars are from radiation burns.

71 Fudschijama, Japan, 1952.

72 Rice harvest near Nikko, Japan, 1952.

73 Japan, 1952.

74 Dockyard in Yokohama, Japan, 1951.

75 Japanese children, Tokyo, 1951.

76 A student writing the lettering for a poster, Tokyo, 1951.

77 Japanese student, Tokyo, 1951.

78 Herd of sheep with Hidalgo in the background, Mexico, 1954.

79 South American Indians in the church of Pisac, Peru, 1954. The pictures of the Pisac Indians were taken in connection with a large-scale journey which Bischof planned to make through Central and South America. It was the confrontation with a different culture that occupied Bischof first and foremost, and a definite change in his style is perceptible in these pictures.

80 Indian child on his mother's back, Peru, 1954.

81–82 Easter procession in Pisac, Peru, 1954.

83 Indian girl with llama herd, Pisac, Peru, 1954.

84 Child's burial, Mexico, 1954.

85 Flute player near Cuzco, Peru, 1954.

Exhibitions

1955 "Japan" (after the book of the same name), Chicago Art Institute. The second version of an exhibition organized by the Traveling Exhibition Department of the Smithsonian Institution.

1956 Retrospectives, Kunstgewerbeschule, Zurich.

1959 "Ten Years of Photography," Eastman House, Rochester, N.Y.

1960 "Magnum 1960," Japan.

1961 Smithsonian Institution, Washington, D.C.

1967 Louvre, Paris.

1967 "The Concerned Photographer" (one of six exhibitions), Riverside Museum, New York, N.Y.

1968 IBM Gallery, New York, N.Y.

1968–1969 Tokyo and other Japanese towns.

1969 Smithsonian Institution, Washington, D.C.

Permanent Public Collections

Art Institute of Chicago
Metropolitan Museum of Art, New York
Museum of Modern Art, New York
Stedelijk Museum, Amsterdam
Kunstgewerbemuseum, Prague
Musée Réattu, Arles

Books

24 Photos von Werner Bischof, text by Manuel Gasser, Kohler Publishers, Berne, Switzerland, 1946.
Japan, text by Robert Guillain, Manesse Publishers, Zurich, 1954.
American edition: Simon & Schuster, New York, 1954.
French edition: Delpire, Paris.
Italian edition: Garzanti, Milan.
English edition: Sylvan Press, London.
Unterwegs, text by Manuel Gasser, Manesse Publishers, Zurich, 1957.
American edition: E. P. Dutton, New York, 1959.
French edition: Delpire, Paris.
Indios, with pictures by other photographers, text by Georges Arnaud, Manesse Publishers, Zurich, 1961. Original publishers: Delpire, Paris.
Werner Bischof, Querschnitt, text by various authors, Arche Publishers, Zurich, 1961.
American edition: Grossman Publishers, New York, 1968. A Polish edition of the work appeared in 1964, edited by Anna Farowa.
The Concerned Photographer, with photographs by other photographers, edited by Cornell Capa, text by various authors, Grossman Publishers, New York, 1968.

Articles

1942 *Du,* "Der invalide Mensch" (The Disabled Human Being)
1944 *Du,* April
1945 *Du,* December, "Refugees"
1948 *Life,* "Winter Olympic Games," St. Moritz
1949 *Du,* June, "Eastern Europe Today"
1949 *Picture Post* (permanent collaboration)
Illustrated (permanent collaboration)
Observer (permanent collaboration)
1950 *Epoca,* Milan; *Life* ("Eastern Europe Today")
1951 *Life* (Starvation in India)
1952 *Paris Match* (Japan; war in Indochina)
1953 *Du,* July, special issue, "People in the Far East"
Fortune
1954 *Life*
1955 *Picture History of Photography,* Peter Pollack
U.S. Camera Annual
Modern Photography
1956 *Camera Magazine*
1957 *ASMP Annual*

1958 *Picture History of Photography,* Helmut Gernsheim

Biographies in Brief

Werner Bischof
Born on April 26, 1916, in Zurich, Switzerland.
1922 Primary and secondary schools in Waldshut.
1931 Interest in painting, attendance at teachers' college in Schiers.
1932 Studies in Schiers interrupted, enrollment at the Kunstgewerbeschule, Zurich. Attendance at Hans Finsler's photography class.
1936 Works as freelance photographer and graphic artist after completion of studies and military training.
1938 Employment with Graphis Publishers, Zurich.
1939 Moves to Paris shortly before the outbreak of war with a view to becoming a painter. Returns to Switzerland, immediately called up into the army.
1942–1944 Publication of photographs in the magazine *Du;* becomes a member of the editorial committee as a permanent collaborator.
1945 Travels through the devastated areas of France, Germany, and Holland with his friend and colleague Emil Schulthess. Publication of a special issue of *Du* on the theme of "Refugees."
1946–1947 Travels through Italy and Greece for the Don Suisse.
1948 Reportage on the Winter Olympic Games in St. Moritz for *Life;* travels in Hungary, Czechoslovakia, Poland, Finland, Sweden, and Denmark.
1949 Contracts with *Picture Post, Illustrated,* and *Observer;* becomes a member of Magnum.
1950 Travels in Italy, Sardinia, Paris; works for the Italian magazine *Epoca.*
1951 Travels through northern and central India and the starvation area of Bihar for *Life.*
1952 After a two-month stay in Japan, interrupted by three journeys to Korea, works in Hong Kong, subsequent war reportages in Indochina for *Paris Match.*
1953 Special issue of *Du:* "People in the Far East," with his pictures of Asia. After making a reportage of the coronation of Queen Elizabeth II of England, travels in the U.S.A., works for *Fortune.*
1954 Travels in Mexico and works in Panama for *Life.* Fatally injured in an accident in Peru when his car plunged into a gorge in the Andes.

Niklaus Flüeler

Born on April 2, 1934, in Lucerne, Switzerland. Educated in Lucerne and Zurich, and finally in Engelberg. Matura examination in 1954. Apprenticeship for one year in a printing office with a view to becoming a publisher. From 1955 to 1962, studied medieval history, German literature, business administration, and journalism at Zurich University and the St. Gall Commercial College, and did practical work as a journalist. Completion of studies at Zurich University in 1962 with a scientific-historical thesis. From 1963 to 1967, jack-of-all-trades in a publishing firm, subsequently one-and-a-half unhappy years in an advertising agency. Since 1969, freelance journalist, designer of books and exhibitions. From December 1969, also editorial collaborator of the *Tagesanzeiger-Magazin* in Zurich.

Romeo E. Martinez

As editor of this series, Romeo E. Martinez crowns an almost 40-year career as journalist and picture director. Martinez was chief of the illustration departments with the magazines *Vu* and *Excelsior* in Paris and is a member of the *Conseil en illustrations de la "Grande Encyclopédie française."* His ten years as editor-in-chief of the monthly magazine *Camera* in Lucerne contributed greatly to the international success of this journal. He has been responsible for the organization of the biennial of photography in Venice.

Index